My name is

_____

I am _____ years old

and in _____ grade

My best friend is

_____

I live in Texas: yes   no

I have lived here for _____

Sleeping Bear Press™

315 E. Eisenhower Parkway, Suite 200
Ann Arbor MI 48108
www.sleepingbearpress.com

Sleeping Bear Press is an imprint of Gale, a part of Cengage Learning.

10 9 8 7 6 5 4 3 2 1

ISBN 978-1-58536-608-8

Printed by China Translation & Printing Services Limited, Guangdong
Province, China. 1st printing.   01/2011

Diary of a Texas Kid

Artwork by Cyd Moore

Where do you live in Texas?

Your address, town/city, and phone number:

_____

_____

_____

Can you walk to school from your house?

_____

_____

How far away from you do your friends live?

_____

_____

Do you have any parks nearby?

_____

_____

Your favorite thing about your neighborhood is:

_____

_____

New Mexico

Amarillo

Oklahoma

Lubbock

Wichita Falls

Fort Worth · Dallas

Odessa

El Paso

Pecos

Arkansas

TEXAS

Waco

Austin

Port Arthur

Houston

Mexico

San Antonio

galves

Corpus Christi

Gulf of Mexico

Laredo

Brownsville

25 MPH

Where Do YOU Live?

WRITE!

Today's date: _____

_____

_____

_____

_____

_____

_____

_____

_____

_____

_____

_____

_____

_____

_____

DRAW!

Today's date: _____

The great state of Texas!

Are you a Texas kid?
How many state facts do
you already know? See if you
can fill in the right answers!
(The correct answers are at the bottom on the next page.)

State bird:

_____

State gemstone:

_____

State flower:

_____

State plant:

_____

State fruit:

_____

State vegetable:

State fish:

State insect:

State song:

State capital:

State nickname:

Bird: Mockingbird • *Gemstone:* Texas Blue Topaz
Flower: Bluebonnet • *Plant:* Prickly Pear Cactus
Fruit: Texas Red Grapefruit • *Vegetable:* Sweet Onion
Fish: Guadalupe Bass • *Insect:* Monarch Butterfly
Song: "Texas, Our Texas" • *Capital:* Austin
Nickname: Lone Star State

WRITE!

Today's date: _____

_____

_____

_____

_____

_____

_____

_____

_____

_____

_____

_____

_____

_____

_____

_____

DRAW!

Today's date: _____

Today we went to

_____

_____

_____

_____

My favorite thing about today was

_____

_____

_____

_____

_____

_____

_____

_____

_____

My least favorite thing about today was

_____

_____

_____

_____

_____

_____

_____

_____

Would I visit here again? Why or why not?

_____

_____

_____

_____

_____

_____

WRITE!

Today's date: _____

_____

_____

_____

_____

_____

_____

_____

_____

_____

_____

_____

_____

_____

_____

Today's date: _____

Did you know that the pecan tree is the state tree of Texas?

Pecan trees grow all over the great state of Texas, especially near the state's rivers, streams, and creeks. There are also pecan orchards located throughout Texas where pecans are grown and sold to make yummy treats like butter pecan ice cream, pecan pie, and even sugar coated pecans!

Make your own pecan brittle!

Ingredients
- 1¼ cups chopped pecans
- 1 cup sugar
- ½ cup light corn syrup
- ⅛ teaspoon salt
- 1 tablespoon butter or margarine
- 1 teaspoon vanilla extract
- 1 teaspoon baking soda

Directions:
Always ask an adult for help in the kitchen before beginning. Combine sugar, salt, and corn syrup in glass mixing bowl, and stir well. Microwave on high for 3 to 4 minutes. Watch closely because microwave oven temperatures can vary. Stir in pecans, then microwave on high for 5 to 6 minutes, until lightly brown. Stir in butter and vanilla. Microwave for 1 more minute. Stir in baking soda. Pour mixture onto a greased cookie sheet, or aluminum foil, and let cool. Break into pieces.

Would you like to try and make pecan popcorn?

It's easy and tasty, especially while your favorite movie is playing!

Ingredients:
- 9 cups popped popcorn (about ⅓ to ½ cup of unpopped kernels before popping)
- ⅔ cup pecan pieces
- 2 tablespoons butter or margarine
- ⅓ cup light corn syrup
- ¼ cup instant dry butter pecan pudding mix
- ½ teaspoon vanilla

Directions:
Always ask an adult for help in the kitchen before beginning. In a small saucepan melt the margarine or butter. Remove saucepan from heat. Stir in the light corn syrup, pudding mix, and vanilla extract. Pour syrup mixture over popcorn and pecans. With a large spoon, gently toss the popped popcorn with the syrup mixture to coat. Bake popcorn, uncovered, in a 300 degree oven for 12-15 minutes, stirring halfway through baking. Using potholders, carefully remove the pan from the oven. Turn mixture onto a large piece of foil. Let popcorn cool completely. Break into bite-sized pieces and serve.

What is your favorite pecan treat to make?

WRITE!

Today's date: _____

DRAW!

Today's date: _____

27

"Remember the Alamo!"

The Battle of the Alamo in 1836 is one of the greatest events in Texas history. During the Texas Revolution against Mexico, Texas soldiers were trapped and outnumbered by the Mexican army in an old mission site called The Alamo. The battle lasted for eleven long days, and then on April 21 the battle cry "Remember the Alamo" inspired the Texas soldiers to defeat the Mexican army and gain independence for Texas.

The Battle of the Alamo also introduced unforgettable characters that would forever be tied with Texas and independence, including James Bowie and David (Davy) Crockett.

Do you know of any other important events in Texas history like the Battle of the Alamo?

_____

_____

_____

_____

_____

_____

_____

_____

WRITE!

Today's date: _____

_____

_____

_____

_____

_____

_____

_____

_____

_____

_____

_____

_____

_____

_____

DRAW!

Today's date: _____

Let's play some games!

Going on a trip?

Here are some fun games to play on your next road trip.

Scavenger Hunt

Before you start out on your trip, make a list of items and places you might see along the way (11 blue cars, 2 bridges, 5 motels, 3 towns that have 10 letters in their names, etc.). Check them off as you find them.

What is the funniest town name you've ever heard?

_____

_____

_____

_____

If you were going to name a town, what would it be?

_____

_____

License Plate Game

Make a list of all the states. See how many different state license plates you can find, and check them off your list. (Variation: Keep a list of all the vanity plates you find.)

Make up your own funny license plates.

Auto Tag

Each person chooses a symbol or something you are likely to encounter regularly on the road, such as a gas station logo, a restaurant sign, a farm animal, a motorcycle. When a player sees her item, she calls it out and gently tags the next player, who then proceeds to search for his symbol, and so on.

35

WRITE!

Today's date: _____

_____

_____

_____

_____

_____

_____

_____

_____

_____

_____

_____

_____

_____

_____

_____

_____

_____

_____

DRAW!

Today's date: _____

Today we went to

_____

_____

_____

_____

_____

My favorite thing about today was

_____

_____

_____

_____

_____

_____

_____

_____

_____

_____

_____

40

My least favorite thing about today was

_____

_____

_____

_____

_____

_____

_____

_____

Would I visit here again? Why or why not?

_____

_____

_____

_____

_____

WRITE!

Today's date: _____

_____

_____

_____

_____

_____

_____

_____

_____

_____

_____

_____

_____

_____

_____

_____

_____

_____

DRAW!

Today's date: _____

Let's GROW something!

Grow a Pizza Garden!

Start plants indoors in early spring, then transfer to pots or the ground outside once they've sprouted and there is no longer danger of frost.

You'll need to grow:

HERBS:

- basil and oregano

VEGETABLES for SAUCE and TOPPINGS:

- tomatoes and bell peppers

What is your very favorite kind of pizza?

_____

_____

_____

_____

_____

_____

...Now...Let's COOK something!

Making a homemade pizza!

FOR YOUR CRUST:

You can use your favorite pizza-dough recipe, or a store-bought pizza crust, or even English muffin halves or tortillas for your crust.

MAKING FRESH PIZZA SAUCE:

Wash and cut as many tomatoes as you like into chunks.
Wash and dry a good handful each of basil and oregano, and chop.

In a saucepan over medium heat, sauté chopped onion and garlic in a small amount of butter or vegetable oil. If you like your sauce spicy, add crushed red pepper next. Now add the tomatoes and herbs and allow the mixture to come to a boil. Turn down the heat to a simmer, stirring occasionally, and let the sauce simmer until most of the liquid has cooked out.

Take sauce off the stove and use either a container blender or a hand-held blender to purée the sauce. Put sauce back on the heat, let it come to a boil again, then allow to simmer until it is the consistency you like.

Let it cool, then spread on pizza dough, or store in the fridge for another time.

ASSEMBLING YOUR PIZZA:

Spread sauce over pizza dough. Top with your chopped, fresh-picked peppers, and any other fresh veggies or meats you like. Now sprinkle cheese over everything and bake in the oven according to your pizza dough recipe. Yum! A homegrown pizza!

WRITE!

Today's date: _____

_____

_____

_____

_____

DRAW!

Today's date: _____

for dinner
this week I had:

Sunday: _____

Monday: _____

Tuesday: _____

Wednesday: _____

Thursday: _____

Friday: _____

Saturday: _____

_____

Favorite movie

_____
_____
_____

Favorite TV show

_____
_____
_____

Favorite video game

_____
_____
_____

Favorite book

_____
_____
_____

Favorite art projects

_____
_____
_____

WRITE!

Today's date: _____

DRAW!

Today's date: _____

Today we went to

My favorite thing about today was

58

My least favorite thing about today was

_____

_____

_____

_____

_____

_____

Would I visit here again? Why or why not?

_____

_____

_____

_____

_____

_____

WRITE!

Today's date: _____

_____

_____

_____

_____

_____

_____

_____

_____

_____

_____

_____

_____

_____

_____

_____

DRAW!

Today's date: _____

Today we went to

_____

_____

_____

_____

My favorite thing about today was

_____

_____

_____

_____

_____

_____

_____

_____

_____

_____

_____

My least favorite thing about today was

_____

_____

_____

_____

_____

_____

_____

Would I visit here again? Why or why not?

_____

_____

_____

_____

_____

WRITE!

Today's date: _____

_____

_____

_____

_____

_____

_____

_____

_____

_____

_____

_____

_____

_____

_____

_____

_____

DRAW!

Today's date: _____

69

Let's play MORE GAMES!

Billboard Poetry

1. Take turns choosing four words from road signs.
2. Give those words to another player who will have one minute to turn the words into a four-line rhyming poem using one word per line.

Eating the Alphabet Game

To start, the first player says, "I'm so hungry I could eat an apple" (or anteater, or alligator). The second player then has to choose something beginning with the next letter of the alphabet, adding to the first player's choice: "I'm so hungry I could eat an apple and a balloon," and so on. See if your family can make it to Z, with each player remembering all the items that came before: "apple, balloon...zebra!"

What is your favorite food?

_____

_____

_____

Can you think of some of your own fun games to play?

_____

_____

_____

_____

_____

_____

_____

_____

WRITE!

Today's date: _____

_____

_____

_____

_____

_____

_____

_____

_____

_____

_____

_____

_____

_____

_____

_____

_____

DRAW!

Today's date: _____

Today we went to

_____

_____

_____

_____

_____

My favorite thing about today was

_____

_____

_____

_____

_____

_____

_____

_____

_____

_____

My least favorite thing about today was

_____

_____

_____

_____

_____

_____

_____

_____

Would I visit here again? Why or why not?

_____

_____

_____

_____

_____

77

WRITE!

Today's date: _____

_____

_____

_____

_____

_____

_____

_____

_____

_____

_____

_____

_____

_____

_____

_____

_____

DRAW!

Today's date: _____

Let's go CAMPING!

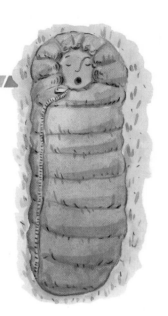

Have you ever gone camping? You can go camping in your own backyard. If it's too cold to camp outside, how about camping in your living room? You can even make s'mores in the kitchen oven!

Write about your camping experiences, or where you hope to go camping someday.

Outside and Inside S'mores

You'll need

Marshmallows
Graham crackers, broken in halves
Chocolate bars, broken in halves
A long stick or skewer for campfire s'mores, or
a baking sheet and aluminum foil for indoor s'mores

HOW TO MAKE CAMPFIRE S'MORES

Get your graham crackers and chocolate ready first.
Lay a chocolate bar half on one graham cracker half and have another
graham cracker half ready to go. Now put a marshmallow on the end of
your stick and hold over the fire, turning to keep it browning nicely and
evenly on all sides. It's finished when it's brown all over and a little crispy
on the outside. Now have a friend sandwich the marshmallow between
the graham and chocolate halves while you pull your stick out of the
marshmallow. Now you have a s'more!

HOW TO MAKE S'MORES IN THE OVEN

Heat oven to 350 degrees. Line a baking sheet with foil. Lay cracker halves
on baking sheet, top with chocolate bar halves, then marshmallows. Toast in
oven for about 5 minutes, just until marshmallow is melty and chocolate
begins to soften. Remove from oven and top with another graham cracker
half. S'mores indoors all year round!

WRITE!

Today's date: _____

_____

_____

_____

_____

_____

_____

_____

_____

_____

_____

_____

_____

_____

_____

_____

_____

DRAW!

Today's date: _____

When I grow up I want to be

A place I hope to go someday

WRITE!

Today's date: _____

_____

_____

_____

_____

_____

_____

_____

_____

_____

_____

_____

_____

_____

_____

DRAW!

Today's date: _____

If I wrote a book it would be about

_____

_____

_____

_____

_____

_____

_____

_____

_____

If I made a movie, it would be about

_____

_____

If I made a TV show, it would be about

_____

_____

If I could star in a movie, I would star as a

_____

_____

If I could star in a TV show, I would star as a

_____

_____

I think it would be fun to be an actor because

_____

_____

95

WRITE!

Today's date: _____

_____

_____

_____

_____

_____

_____

_____

_____

_____

_____

_____

_____

_____

_____

_____

_____

DRAW!

Today's date: _____

Today we went to

_____

_____

_____

_____

My favorite thing about today was

_____

_____

_____

_____

_____

_____

_____

My least favorite thing about today was

_____

_____

_____

_____

_____

_____

_____

_____

Would I visit here again? Why or why not?

_____

_____

_____

_____

_____

_____

WRITE!

Today's date: _____

DRAW!

Today's date: _____

105

What do you love about going back to school?

School days

My favorite subject in school

_____

_____

_____

My least favorite subject in school

_____

_____

_____

If I were a teacher, I would

_____

_____

_____

If I could change one thing about school, I would

_____

_____

_____

The thing I like most about school

_____

_____

WRITE!

Today's date: _____

_____

_____

_____

_____

_____

_____

_____

_____

_____

_____

_____

_____

_____

_____

_____

 DRAW!

Today's date: _____

WRITE!

Today's date: _____

_____

_____

_____

_____

_____

_____

_____

_____

_____

_____

_____

_____

_____

_____

_____

A place I hope to go someday

_____

_____

If I could live anywhere in the world I'd choose

_____

_____

Someone I wish lived near me

_____

_____

Of all the places I've been, I liked this best

_____

_____

Of all the places I've been, I really didn't like

_____

_____

If I could change one thing
about where I live it would be

_____

_____

_____

_____

_____

_____

_____

_____

_____

115

WRITE!

Today's date: _____

_____

_____

_____

_____

_____

_____

_____

_____

_____

_____

_____

_____

_____

_____

_____

_____

DRAW!

Today's date: _____

Can you write your own poem? Here's how.

1st Stanza

I am.. (*two special characteristics you have*)

I wonder .... (*something you are actually curious about*)

I hear .... (*an imaginary sound*)

I see .... (*an imaginary sight*)

I want... (*an actual desire*)

I am.. (*the first line of the poem repeated*)

2nd Stanza

I pretend................................ (*something you actually pretend to do*)

I feel .... (*a feeling about something imaginary*)

I touch... (*an imaginary touch*)

I worry .... (*something that really bothers you*)

I cry.............................(*something that makes you very sad*)

I am............................ (*the first line of the poem repeated*)

3rd Stanza

I understand .... (*something you know is true*)

I say...(*something you believe in*)

I dream.................................. (*something you actually dream about*)

I try.............................(*something you really make an effort about*)

I hope................................. (*something you actually hope for*)

I am.. (*the first line of the poem repeated*)

Now, write your own poem here:

1st Stanza

I am _____

I wonder _____

I hear_____

I see _____

I want _____

I am _____

2nd Stanza

I pretend_____

I feel_____

I touch _____

I worry_____

I cry _____

I am _____

3rd Stanza

I understand _____

I say _____

I dream _____

I try _____

I hope_____

I am _____

WRITE!

Today's date: _____

_____

_____

_____

_____

_____

_____

_____

_____

_____

_____

_____

_____

_____

_____

DRAW!

Today's date: _____

The success of Texas: Cattle and Sheep!

Texas is known for its cattle ranching and agricultural lifestyle. In fact, the famous and historical King Ranch located in Kingsville, Texas is bigger than the state of Rhode Island—really!

In addition to cattle ranching, Texas is also at the top of the list in the production of wool. Did you know that wool comes from the woolen fleece of sheep—it's true! This practice is called sheep shearing. Once the wool of a sheep reaches a certain length, it is shaved off so the sheep is ready to grow more wool that's used to make clothes and to be spun into yarn.

Baa!

Try a stick weaving craft with yarn.

What you will need:

- Yarn (at least two colors)
- Scissors
- 2 small craft sticks

1.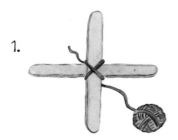

1. Tie the craft sticks together by crisscrossing the yarn in an "X" shape several times in the middle. Tie the yarn into a knot in the back. Now you are ready to weave.

2.

2. To begin weaving, wrap the yarn over and around one stick, then over and around the next, over and around the next, and so on until the craft sticks are about half covered.

3.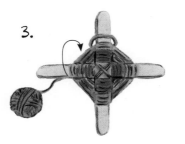

3. Next, tie a different colored piece of yarn onto one of the sticks, and begin weaving the yarn around the sticks as you did before. Stop about ¼ inch from the ends of the sticks.

4.

4. Complete by cutting the yarn (leaving about 7 to 8 inches), making a knot in the end of the yarn, and tucking it under the last stitch you wrapped.

What makes YOU a Texas kid?